Drawing Is Fun!

DRAWING
WILD ANIMALS

Gareth Stevens
Publishing

Please visit our Web site, www.garethstevens.com. For a free color catalog of all our high-quality books, call toll free 1-800-542-2595 or fax 1-877-542-2596.

Library of Congress Cataloging-in-Publication Data

Cook, Trevor, 1948-
Drawing wild animals / Trevor Cook and Lisa Miles.
    p. cm. — (Drawing is fun!)
Includes index.
ISBN 978-1-4339-5079-7 (pbk.)
ISBN 978-1-4339-5080-3 (6-pack)
ISBN 978-1-4339-5032-2 (library binding)
1. Animals in art—Juvenile literature. 2. Wildlife art—Juvenile literature. 3. Drawing—Technique—Juvenile literature. I. Miles, Lisa. II. Title.
NC780.C665 2011
743.6—dc22

                                        2010027763

First Edition

Published in 2011 by
Gareth Stevens Publishing
111 East 14th Street, Suite 349
New York, NY 10003

Copyright © 2011 Arcturus Publishing

Artwork: Q2A India
Text: Trevor Cook and Lisa Miles
Editors: Fiona Tulloch and Joe Harris
Cover design: Akihiro Nakayama

Picture credits: All photographs supplied by Shutterstock.

Printed in the United States

CPSIA compliance information: Batch #AW11GS: For further information contact Gareth Stevens, New York, New York at 1-800-542-2595.

SL001768US

Contents

Camel

Long eyelashes protect the camel's eyes from sand.

His hump stores fat.

This camel has one hump, but some types have two humps.

He has wide, padded feet for walking on soft sand.

FUN FACTS ● FUN FACTS ● FUN FACTS ● FUN FACTS ● FUN FACTS

If a camel doesn't eat for a while, the fat in its hump is used up. The hump goes all floppy!

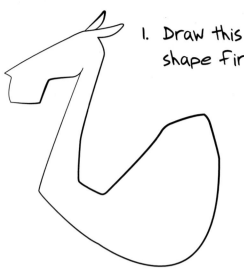

1. Draw this shape first.

2. Now put in a front and a back leg.

3. Add the other legs.

4. He's got a hairy hump and a hairy chin.

Dolphin

A dolphin's shape helps him to swim fast.

The dolphin is a playful animal. He jumps through the waves for fun.

He has small, sharp teeth.

Dolphins swim together in groups. The groups are called pods.

FUN FACTS ● FUN FACTS ● FUN FACTS ● FUN FACTS ● FUN FACTS

Dolphins like to talk to each other. They make clicking and whistling sounds.

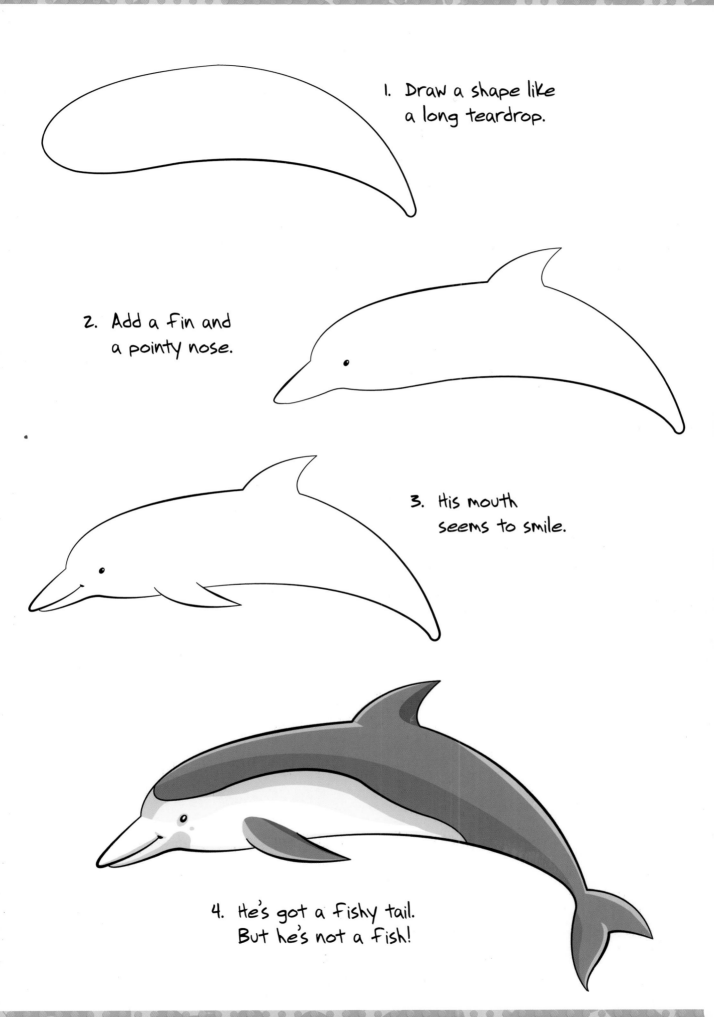

1. Draw a shape like a long teardrop.

2. Add a fin and a pointy nose.

3. His mouth seems to smile.

4. He's got a fishy tail. But he's not a fish!

Lion

A lion has thick hair around his neck. This is called a mane.

The lion hunts other animals for food. He has excellent eyesight.

A lion is about as long as a man lying down.

His claws are very sharp.

FUN FACTS ● FUN FACTS ● FUN FACTS ● FUN FACTS ● FUN FACTS

Lions roar to communicate with each other. A lion's roar can be heard five miles (eight km) away. That's loud!

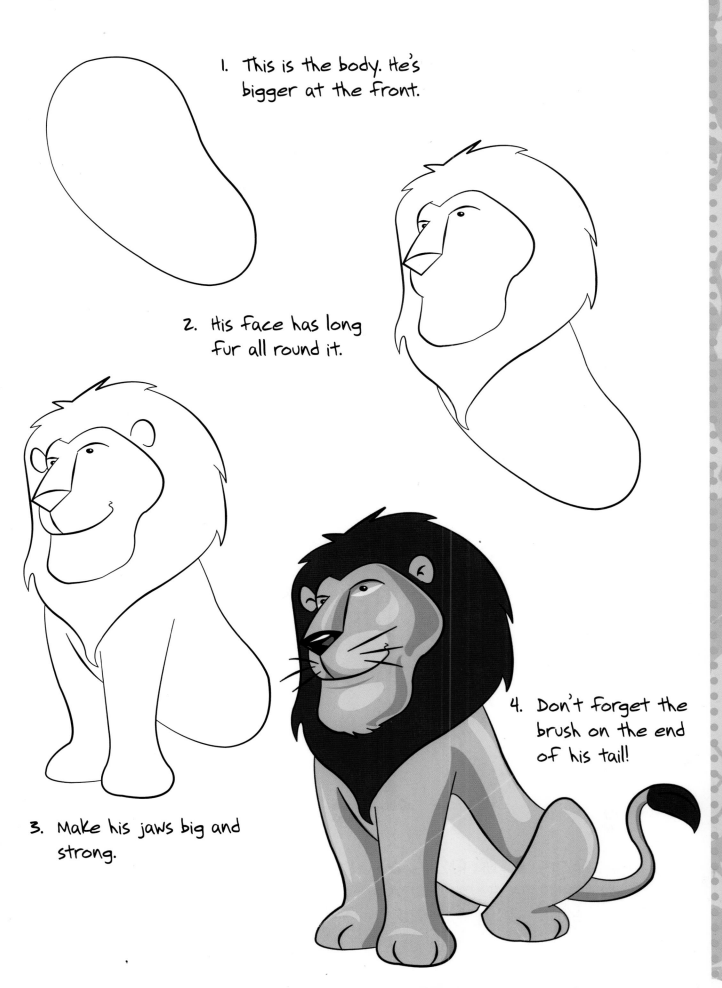

1. This is the body. He's bigger at the front.

2. His face has long fur all round it.

3. Make his jaws big and strong.

4. Don't forget the brush on the end of his tail!

Giraffe

The giraffe is the tallest animal.

She eats leaves from tall trees.

Giraffes have spots on their coats. Each giraffe has a different spotty pattern.

Giraffes sleep for two hours each day. Sometimes they nap standing up.

FUN FACTS ● FUN FACTS ● FUN FACTS ● FUN FACTS ● FUN FACTS

A father giraffe is called a bull. A mother is called a cow. A baby is called a calf!

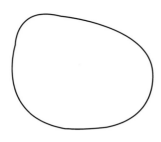

1. Her body is quite small.

2. Make her neck long and curvy.

3. Give her four strong legs.

4. She has a special pattern on her coat.

Rhinoceros

Rhinos have excellent hearing. However they cannot see very well.

Some kinds of rhino have one horn. Others have two.

Rhinos have very thick skin.

They can run as fast as a racing bicycle.

FUN FACTS ● FUN FACTS ● FUN FACTS ● FUN FACTS ● FUN FACTS

The rhino is the second largest land animal. Only the elephant is bigger!

1. Draw a body like a big rock.

2. His face is low down.

3. Give him little ears and eyes. Add a strong horn on his nose.

4. Draw his four legs. He's got lumpy knees!

Gorilla

A gorilla is very heavy. He weighs almost as much as three men!

The gorilla is a gentle animal.

His body is covered in lots of black fur.

He can stand on two legs. However he likes to move on all fours.

FUN FACTS ● FUN FACTS ● FUN FACTS ● FUN FACTS ● FUN FACTS

A group of gorillas is called a troop. The leader is a male called a silverback. He has silver hair on his back!

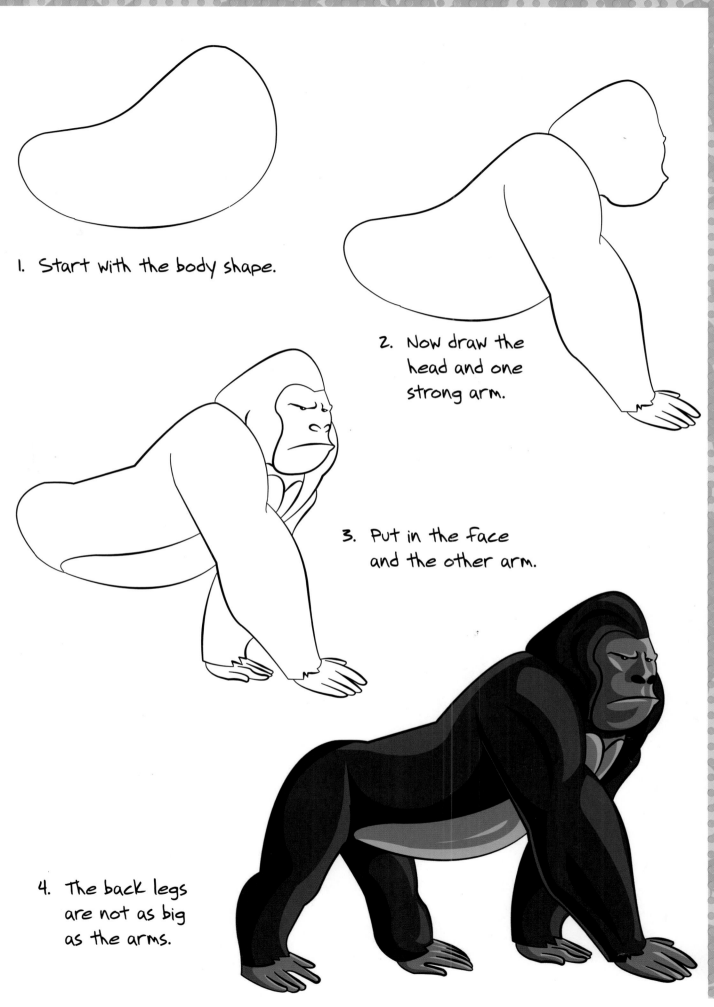

1. Start with the body shape.

2. Now draw the head and one strong arm.

3. Put in the face and the other arm.

4. The back legs are not as big as the arms.

Leopard

The leopard has a spotty coat. She can hide in the trees and grass.

Her long tail helps her to balance.

She has strong legs. She's a fast runner and a good swimmer, too!

She has soft pads on her paws. These help her to walk quietly.

FUN FACTS ● FUN FACTS ● FUN FACTS ● FUN FACTS ● FUN FACTS

A leopard often drags its food up a tree to eat it. It can pull up to three times its own body weight!

1. Draw this sausage shape.

2. Draw the head with an open mouth.

3. Now add the front legs and tail.

4. Put on her back legs and her special spotty pattern.

Shark

This shark is called a gray reef shark.

He has very sharp teeth. He kills other animals for food.

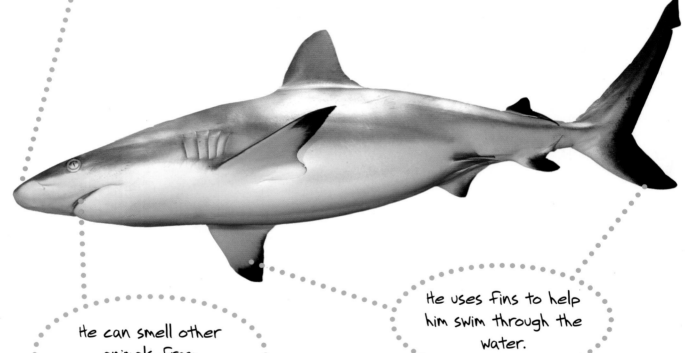

He can smell other animals from far away.

He uses fins to help him swim through the water.

FUN FACTS ● FUN FACTS ● FUN FACTS ● FUN FACTS ● FUN FACTS

The biggest fish in the ocean is the whale shark. It's longer than a bus!

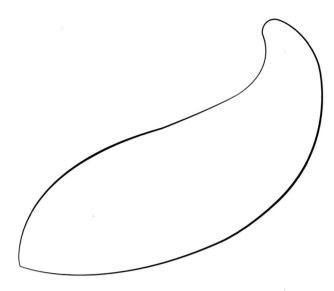

1. Make the body curvy.

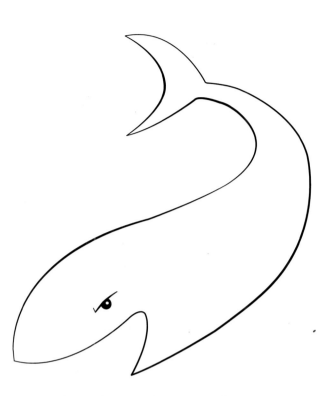

2. Give him a big mouth and an angry eye.

3. The fins and tail are pointed.

4. Finish him off with sharp teeth.

Tiger

The tiger is the largest cat.

His stripes help him to hide in the trees. Most tigers have more than 100 stripes.

He has long front teeth for biting.

He has strong paws with long claws.

FUN FACTS ● FUN FACTS ● FUN FACTS ● FUN FACTS ● FUN FACTS

Most tigers are orange with black stripes. Sometimes, a tiger is born that is white with black stripes!

1. Copy this shape carefully.

2. Make his eyes scowl.

3. His face is really fierce.

4. Finish him off with tiger stripes.

Polar bear

The polar bear is the biggest meat-eater on land.

His claws help him to catch animals. They also stop him falling over on the ice.

He lives in the far north. It is very cold there. His fur keeps him warm.

His fur is white, like the snow.

FUN FACTS ● FUN FACTS ● FUN FACTS ● FUN FACTS ● FUN FACTS

Under the polar bear's white fur, it has black skin!

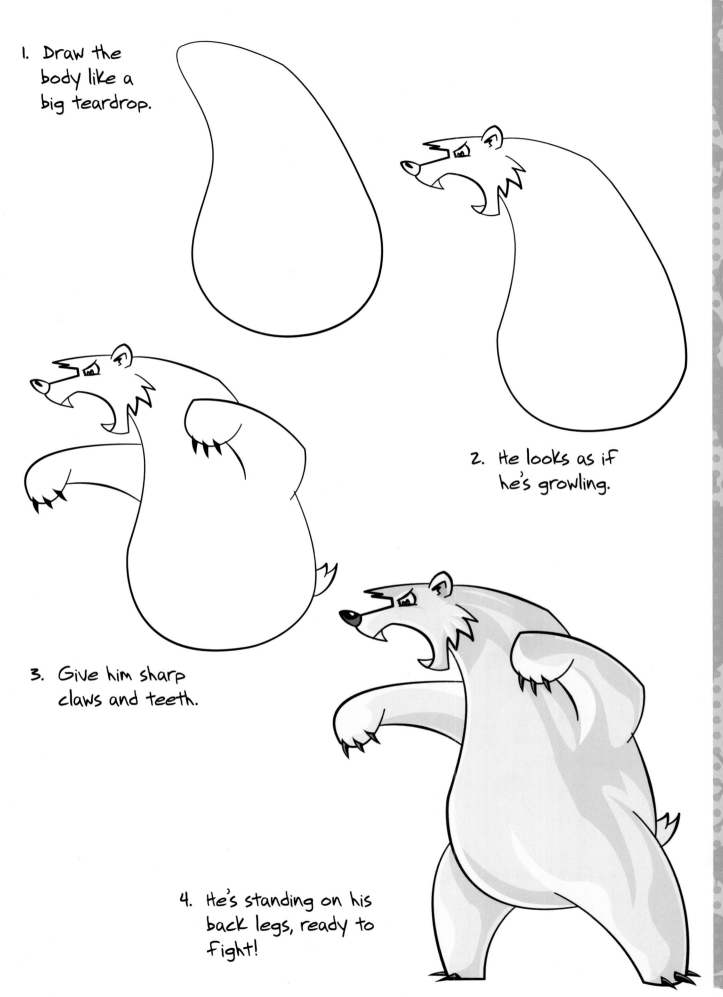

1. Draw the body like a big teardrop.

2. He looks as if he's growling.

3. Give him sharp claws and teeth.

4. He's standing on his back legs, ready to fight!

Elephant

He has a long, curly tooth called a tusk.

The elephant flaps his ears to keep cool.

He uses his long trunk like a hand for picking things up.

He needs thick, strong legs because he is so heavy.

FUN FACTS ● FUN FACTS ● FUN FACTS ● FUN FACTS ● FUN FACTS

The elephant is the largest animal that lives on land. It weighs nine tons (8,000 kg).

1. Begin with a big egg shape.

2. Put in his mouth and his curly trunk ...

3. ... ears, tusks, and some legs.

4. Color him gray and don't forget his tail!

Hippopotamus

The hippopotamus spends a lot of time in the river.

His ears, eyes, and nose are at the top of his head. The rest of his body can stay underwater.

His skin makes its own special sunscreen!

His mouth opens really wide.

FUN FACTS ● FUN FACTS ● FUN FACTS ● FUN FACTS ● FUN FACTS

The hippopotamus can walk underwater. It can hold its breath for up to five minutes!

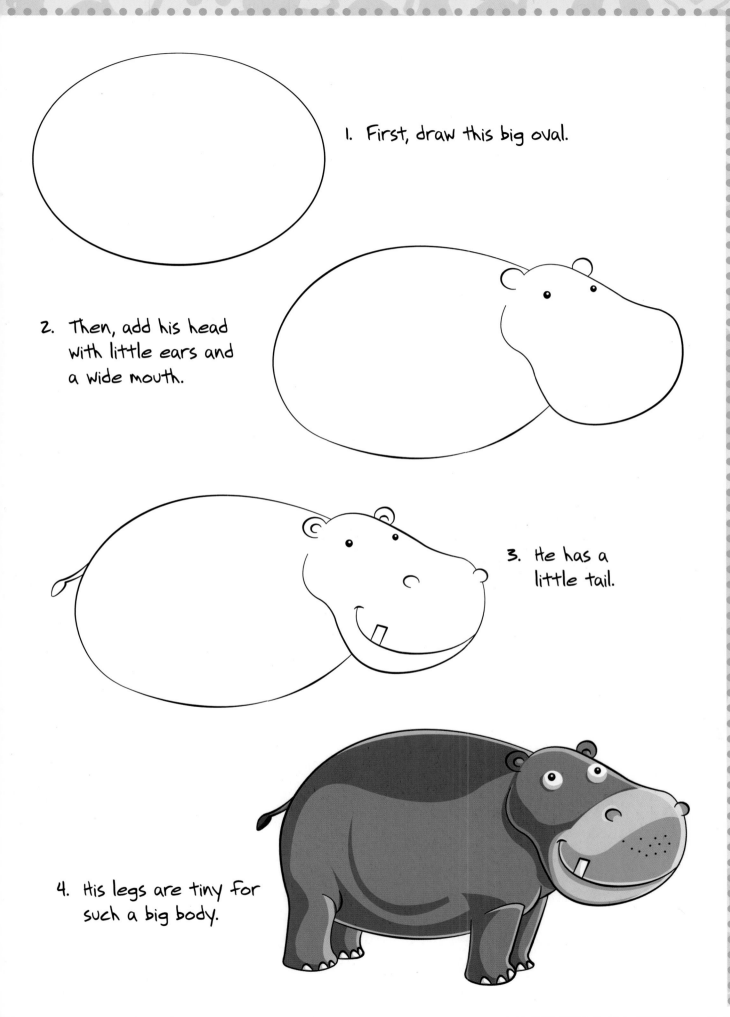

1. First, draw this big oval.

2. Then, add his head with little ears and a wide mouth.

3. He has a little tail.

4. His legs are tiny for such a big body.

orangutan

orangutans like to swing between trees.

An orangutan's arms are long and strong.

She has long fingers. They can hold on tight to branches.

All orangutans have reddish-brown or orange hair.

FUN FACTS ● FUN FACTS ● FUN FACTS ● FUN FACTS ● FUN FACTS

orangutans are very smart. They can even learn to use sign language.

1. Draw this wobbly shape to start.

2. Add the face.

3. Give her long hairy arms.

4. Bananas are her favorite food.

Penguin

There are 17 types of penguin. This is a King penguin.

Penguins are birds but they can't fly! They use their wings to swim.

She has fluffy feathers to keep her warm.

Penguins live in the far south. It's very cold.

FUN FACTS ● FUN FACTS ● FUN FACTS ● FUN FACTS ● FUN FACTS

Penguins can jump out of the water, up into the air!

1. Draw this shape like a pointy egg.

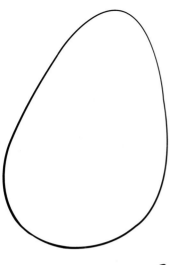

2. Put the head on with its long beak.

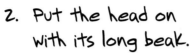

3. Her wings are like flippers.

4. She looks well dressed in black and white.

Glossary

balance stand or move without falling over

coat the fur covering an animal

drag pull along on the ground

eyelashes special hairs that keep dust out of your eyes

fat something oily and squashy which is found inside animals

flipper a flat, long arm or leg without fingers or toes. It is used for swimming.

gentle kind and caring

growl a low noise made by animals when they are angry or scared

hump a bump on an animal's back

mane fur around an animal's neck

oval shaped like an egg

pad a soft piece of skin without fur on an animal's hand or foot

silverback the leader of a group of gorillas

sunscreen a cream that you rub into skin to stop the sun from burning you

teardrop a shape with a point at the top and a round bottom

trunk an elephant's long nose

tusk a long, curling tooth

Further Reading

Green, Dan. *How to Draw 101 Animals*. Top That! Kids, 2004.

Hayashi, Hikaru. *How to Draw Manga Volume 36: Animals*. Graphic-Sha, 2005.

Milbourne, Anna et al. *Drawing Animals*. E.D.C. Publishing, 2002.

Index

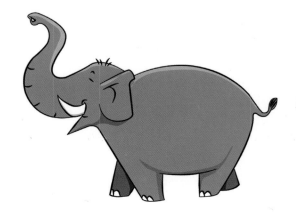